REFLECTIONS FOR OUR
Highs and Lows

MARJA BERGEN

REFLECTIONS FOR OUR HIGHS AND LOWS
Copyright © 2014 Marja Bergen

All rights reserved. Neither this publication nor any part of this publication may be reproduced or transmitted in any form or by any means, electronic or mechanical, including photocopying, recording or any information storage and retrieval system, without permission in writing from the author.

All photography by Marja Bergen.

All Scripture quotations, unless otherwise specified, are taken from the Holy Bible, New International Version®, NIV® Copyright © 1973, 1978, 1984, 2011 by Biblica, Inc.® Used by permission. All rights reserved worldwide.

Scripture quotations marked NIV 1984 are taken from the Holy Bible, NEW INTERNATIONAL VERSION®. Copyright © 1973, 1978, 1984 by Biblica, Inc. All rights reserved worldwide. Used by permission.

Scripture quotations marked NLT are taken from the Holy Bible, New Living Translation copyright© 1996, 2004, 2007 by Tyndale House Foundation. Used by permission of Tyndale House Publishers Inc., Carol Stream, Illinois 60188. All rights reserved.

Scripture quotations marked MSG are taken from The Message, Copyright © 1993, 1994, 1995, 1996, 2000, 2001, 2002 by Eugene H. Peterson.

Scripture quotations marked NIRV are taken from the Holy Bible, New International Reader's Version® Copyright © 1995, 1996, 1998 by Biblica. All rights reserved worldwide.

Printed in Canada

ISBN: 978-1-4866-0231-5

Word Alive Press
131 Cordite Road, Winnipeg, MB R3W 1S1
www.wordalivepress.ca

Cataloguing in Publication may be obtained through Library and Archives Canada

I dedicate this book to two individuals who are very special to me.

I am grateful to Helen Forewell and her brother Pastor Don Dyck for how they have supported me and helped me learn to know God better through their words and action. I don't think I could have written these devotionals if it weren't for these friends' influence on my life.

Contents

The Crocus, My Symbol of Hope	1
Morning Has Broken (poem)	3
Morning Has Broken	4
God is Doing a New Thing	6
This is the Day	8
At the Feet of Jesus	10
Think About Such Things	12
He Will Quiet You	14
Will You Be a Child for Me?	16
The Rat Downstairs	18
A Father's Compassion	20
Broken-Hearted	22
Come and Have Breakfast	24
Do Not Delay, Lord	26
Great is Thy Faithfulness	28
Heaven on Earth	30
How Great His Love	32
How Long, Lord?	34
"I Don't Want to Lie Down!"	36
Light in the Darkness	38
Lighting a Candle in the Night	40
Mystery Tour	42
On Wings Like Eagles	44

Patient Endurance	46
Raindrops on Roses	48
Singing When You Don't Feel Like It	50
Talking to God About Joy	52
The Potter	54
This is Joy	56
Who Am I?	58
Endnotes	61
About the Author	63

The Crocus, My Symbol of Hope

The writings in this little book started out as *Reflections on Scripture*, emails I shared every Monday morning with people, most of whom, like me, have mental health problems. Gradually I began adding my photographs, and these became an important part of the message. Today I share some of my favourites, hoping they will touch your heart. I also hope the Scripture selections will speak to you, encourage and inspire you, as they have me.

You will see many photographs of crocuses throughout this book, and you might wonder why.

When I was beginning work on the book, I bought a little bulb garden in a pot, wanting very much to photograph crocuses. I spent several sessions with the plants, using various locations and using different qualities of light. Gradually they became a symbol to me of the new life we all pray for when we're not doing well. We welcome the end of winter and look forward to spring. Crocuses became a symbol of hope to me.

I pray that God will be a source of hope, strength and comfort as you go through your highs and lows. God says to all of us who struggle with mental health problems,

> *"You matter to me, I love you, I created you, I formed you.*
> *I have a plan for your life greater than the pain you're going through.*
> *You are valuable, you are acceptable, you are lovable,*
> *you are forgivable and you are usable."*[1]

Morning Has Broken

I waited patiently for the Lord;
he turned to me and heard my cry.
He lifted me out of the slimy pit,
out of the mud and mire;
he set my feet on a rock
and gave me a firm place to stand.
He put a new song in my mouth,
a hymn of praise to our God.
Many will see and fear the Lord
and put their trust in him.
Psalm 40:1-3

Morning Has Broken

Sunrise

My favourite place on early spring and summer mornings is in my Muskoka chair on the patio. Nothing makes me happier than to have my first cup of coffee there, my journal and Bible on my lap. I usually get outside while it's still dark, waiting for the sun to rise and the birds to start their chirping. It's the best time of day.

One morning I had my camera out with me, hoping to capture the flock of tiny nuthatches that liked to flit amongst the stems of the daisies only feet away. They didn't appear. But the sunrise didn't let me down. It lit up the daisies and fuchsias beautifully. I played with my camera, trying to photograph the magical scene using various angles and compositions.

Breathless. Exhilarated.

Isn't that how we feel when we awaken after a long period of grief, pain or depression? There's nothing like the relief of knowing we have our lives back, like the sparkling light of a new morning. At least, that's how it is for me as a person living with bipolar disorder.

But oh how patiently we sometimes have to wait for this to happen! How we cry out to the Lord for release from the pain! He *will* come through for us though, eventually. God *will* lift us out of our muddy existence. He *will* once more give us a firm place to stand. As surely as day follows night, our pain will lift. This is God's promise to us if we will trust Him.

Morning will break.

I'm so glad David wrote Psalm 40. It reflects my experience with depression. David understands and it feels good to be understood, especially by a person who was a man after God's own heart.

The intensity, the brilliance and sense of freedom seem like a strange phenomenon after so many dark weeks and months. And yet this is how it is: a fresh new morning after a never-ending night. We can't help but sing a joyous new song of praise to God. And how we'd love to sing it everywhere we go! Our transformation is amazing, yet this is how God works.

God is Doing a New Thing

Cyclamen

Forget the former things; do not dwell on the past. See, I am doing a new thing! Now it springs up; do you not perceive it? I am making a way in the wilderness and streams in the wasteland.

Isaiah 43:18–19

It's a sorry fact that too many of us dwell on things that are long past. Pain, failure and loss play far too big a role in our memory. While it's okay to remember and grieve, God tells us that to dwell on the past is wasting precious today time.

There's nothing we can do to create a better yesterday. But today is another story. Look at what God gives us: sixteen waking hours, ready to make what we wish of them. Sixteen sparklingly, wondrously new hours to work and play. Time to take on delicious challenges. Time to create. Time to enjoy family and friends. Time to give and receive love.

God is doing a new thing.

Wonderful things can happen—and we don't always have to wait for them. If we lean on God, He will lead us. He will help us make things happen. What freedom!

"Now it springs up; do you not perceive it?"

I remember weeks and months spent in the wilderness, unable to find my way out. Such a relief it was when God removed the cobwebs from my confused mind and cleared the way. He helped me see again. He helped me make life happen again.

Can you identify? Have you been in a wasteland far too long? If you have, take heart. God promises us streams of fresh running water. If we put our trust in Him, He will help us turn our desert into a garden, with rich, colourful flowers. Why not start planting today?

"Forget the former things; do not dwell on the past."

This is the Day

This is the day the LORD has made; let us rejoice and be glad in it.
Psalm 118:24, NIV 1984

I have fond memories of singing these words at church as the choir and pastor filed down the aisle in their long blue robes. How glad I was that it was Sunday morning and I was at church, worshipping with my friends! The hymn encouraged my eagerness.

This verse always makes me joyful, reminding me of each new day God has given me.

It's not always easy for me to recognize God's gifts or to feel joy. I've experienced black times when I could not bear the pain, times when I no longer wanted to live. One day I felt a genuine need to ask my pastor why I should live. I really couldn't remember. All joy was gone.

Though it was difficult for me at that time, most people's moods *are* elevated by this verse. Why do these words bring such enthusiasm?

This passage deals with gratitude and joy, two things very much connected.

A fellow patient at a treatment facility I attended recently told me how happy he feels whenever he expresses his gratitude to God. I feel the same way. The Benedictine monk Brother David Steindl-Rast was right when he said, "It is not joy that makes us grateful; it is gratitude that makes us joyful."[2]

Can we bring back joy when we've lost it, simply by expressing gratitude to God? I believe we can, even when life is hard.

There are the obvious things to be grateful for: food on the table, a place to call home, friends and family to love, daisies in the garden. It would take many books to list them all. If you're tempted to think you don't have much to thank God for, consider what you may be taking for granted: legs to walk, hands to work and play, a mouth to speak, ears to hear. You may not always have these, but while you do, they can be a cause for gratitude. Think of each one, and thank God. You may find your joy coming back.

So, what did my pastor say when I asked him to remind me why I should live? He said, "The reason you live is so that you can give others a reason to live."

How that simple sentence lifted me! I'd forgotten that this is what life is about. I'm not living for myself alone. What a relief to remember that. My hope was renewed. Gratitude and joy eventually returned.

With God's help, we can give others a reason to live, just by being who we are, just by being part of their lives and caring for them. In this amazing truth, we can find our life, our gratitude and our joy.

"This is the day the LORD has made; let us rejoice and be glad in it."

At the Feet of Jesus

Crocuses after a frost

A woman in that town who lived a sinful life learned that Jesus was eating at the Pharisee's house, so she came there with an alabaster jar of perfume. As she stood behind him at his feet weeping, she began to wet his feet with her tears. Then she wiped them with her hair, kissed them and poured perfume on them.
Luke 7:37–38

How this woman, believed to be a prostitute, must have loved Jesus! Other people, like the Pharisee, treated her with disdain. But Jesus saw her as a person He could accept and love, in spite of her sins. What a relief that must have been for her.

Where did that weeping come from? Have you ever felt this way?

Her weeping reminds me of how I cried in church when I started following Jesus. Many times I couldn't hold back the tears that flowed inexplicably during the singing of the hymns. I was like a child who had been separated from her mother far too long and was newly returned to her. My tears released my pent-up emotions, relieving the stress of trying to do life on my own. Not knowing the love of Christ had been harder on me than I realized. I was embarrassed to break down like this in church, yet it felt good to let it all out.

I've heard from many who have such emotions surface during worship. Tears in church are not uncommon. But imagine if we could, like this woman, have the physical presence of Jesus right there with us. Imagine if we could also kneel at His feet when the tears come rolling down. The relief! The joy!

But maybe we can do the next best thing. Next time we feel the tears surfacing, we can picture the Lord Jesus close to us. We too can worship at His feet, knowing that we don't have to struggle on our own. We too are loved. We too are forgiven.

Think About Such Things

Do not be anxious about anything, but in every situation, by prayer and petition, with thanksgiving, present your requests to God. And the peace of God, which transcends all understanding, will guard your hearts and your minds in Christ Jesus. Finally, brothers and sisters, whatever is true, whatever is noble, whatever is right, whatever is pure, whatever is lovely, whatever is admirable—if anything is excellent or praiseworthy—think about such things.

Philippians 4:6–8

Long ago, a mass of buttercups grew in a park nearby. How I loved the cheerful blossoms. The humble flowers danced around me as I lay in their midst, photographing them! I found much happiness there.

I need times like that, times when I can focus on positive things, the things I love and am grateful for. I'm not always able to do that. All too often, my mind is drawn to negative thoughts. It's difficult to extract myself.

Can you identify?

Have you ever had times when something triggered intense negative thoughts and feelings? It happens to me quite often. The trigger does not have to be a big deal. Small triggers can cause big feelings.

Maybe you thought you were being ignored during coffee time after church. Your perception may have been unfounded, yet it was real to you. You felt like a social failure. You may have felt unloved or unworthy. And wow! Can those thoughts do a number on you!

This is common for people with mood disorders. You are not alone. These anxieties can cause full-blown depression, and it's important to search for healing promptly. Otherwise, you may have a hard time digging out.

A good friend wisely told me, "Negative thoughts and feelings definitely do *not* come from God." Those simple words help me get through the critical stage. She reminded me that this is not what God is like at all. He loves me, and His love is *always* present, no matter what I feel or think of myself.

The Scripture quoted here, part of Paul's letter to the Philippians, is a treasure. Meditating on verses like these can make the negativity melt away.

Fix your thoughts on what is...pure, and lovely, and admirable.

God calls us all to focus our minds on the good things, though our tendency may be to focus on the bad. It can be so hard to get our minds off the negative! But God can help. He has blessed us with so much—music, books, sunshine, nature, things we enjoy.

What makes us happy? What can we focus on?

He Will Quiet You

Quieted with Love

*The LORD your God is with you, he is mighty to save. He will take great delight in you,
he will quiet you with his love, he will rejoice over you with singing.*
Zephaniah 3:17, NIV 1984

Imagine! Holy God, Creator, the One who is above all, our Father in heaven! Imagine Him rejoicing over us, with all our shortcomings.

I have trouble finding adequate words to describe how amazing this is and what it means for God to sing. So I will quote John Piper in one of his sermons:

> *Can you imagine what it would be like if you could hear God singing?
> Remember that it was merely a spoken word that brought the universe into existence.
> What would happen if God lifted up his voice and not only spoke but sang!*[3]

I held this verse close during a particularly severe depression years ago. But I only hung on to the first and fourth lines: *"The LORD your God is with you…he will quiet you with his love."* I read these lines over and over, finding solace in them. From those words I drew the sustenance I needed.

I couldn't fathom the part about God rejoicing over me—not the way I was feeling. In that dark place, I wasn't in any mood to have anyone, not even God Himself, sing over me. I needed quiet. I needed a soothing of the spirit. It was tremendously reassuring to hear that there was an awesome God loving me and holding me close. The solace I found in His arms during those painful times was a wonderful relief.

Things are different now that I'm no longer in such deep depression. I'm more able to seek the Lord. I'm able to absorb the full message.

And I stand in awe-filled wonder at how God can take delight in us and rejoice over us with song. Who are we, after all, to be considered precious enough for that? God thinks we are.

How He loves us! Every one of us!

Will You Be a Child for Me?

In a wooded campground

People brought babies to Jesus, hoping he might touch them. When the disciples saw it, they shooed them off. Jesus called them back. "Let these children alone. Don't get between them and me. These children are the kingdom's pride and joy. Mark this: Unless you accept God's kingdom in the simplicity of a child, you'll never get in."

Luke 18:15–17 MSG

For many years, I have loved photographing children. Children five and under are my favourites. That's when they can still express themselves freely. Young children are open and real. How precious that is to see!

I photographed this little girl many years ago. She was enraptured by the things she discovered in a wooded campground. Her family had just arrived after a long road trip, and she and her sister had a wonderful time exploring. She found some wild strawberries and held them, as a treasure, in her left hand while admiring the wildflowers close by. Such sweet joy!

What impresses me about young children is their attitude of love for God's creation. When they're exploring new things, they get caught up in the awe of what they see around them. Everything else, every distraction, fades away.

Wouldn't it be nice to live like that? To forget our troubles and give our attention to God's handiwork? I want to be like the child in this picture, openly receiving what God has given me, lost in the wonder of it.

It would be beautiful to keep the curiosity we had as children. How precious to be as delighted as a child, excited about our discoveries!

If only we could hold this attitude of love towards the things God has created! God asks us, "Will you be a child for Me?"

The Rat Downstairs

Deliver me from my enemies, O God; be my fortress against those who are attacking me.
Deliver me from evildoers and save me from those who are after my blood…You are my strength,
I watch for you; you, God, are my fortress, my God on whom I can rely.
Psalm 59:1–2; 9–10

David wrote this psalm when Saul had sent men to his house to kill him. Yes, King David, the man of God, had much cause to be anxious. His life was often in danger. Nevertheless, he trusted God to strengthen him. What a good example he is for us!

Many of us have anxieties—about health, safety, finances, relationships, weight, our future and a myriad other things. These anxieties can keep us from being productive, and they affect our ability to be happy.

What is worrying you? What do you fear? Can you imagine David's situation? Can you, like David, rely on God?

I, too, have had problems with anxiety. I still do. How I wish I could be more like David!

As a young child living in Amsterdam, I was frightened by a rat in the downstairs foyer of our flat. The ugly creature seemed to be coming after me, and I was seized with fear. I ran as quickly as my legs would carry me up the stairs, crying and screaming for my parents.

I didn't leave our flat for many days, afraid I would see the rat again. At the dining-room table, I sat on my knees, not wanting to put my legs under the table. I lived in constant fear, the rat always on my mind. In spite of my parents' coaxing, I would not go downstairs to go outside.

Life isn't fun for an anxious person.

Eventually my father talked me into going out with him. He held my hand firmly as we walked around the neighbourhood. I took big jumps over the gutters, worried that rats might be hiding there. After a while, my self-assurance returned. There were no rats there at all! I was relieved to let go of the fear, happy to have someone trustworthy holding my hand.

That's how it is when we rely on God. We can release the fear and become stronger—free to live with confidence again.

With David, we'll be able to sing, *"But I will sing of your strength, in the morning I will sing of your love; for you are my fortress, my refuge in times of trouble"* (Psalm 59:16).

A Father's Compassion

The Lord said, "I have indeed seen the misery of my people in Egypt. I have heard them crying out because of their slave drivers, and I am concerned about their suffering."
Exodus 3:7

When our son was seven, he took the lid off the pepper shaker and decided to clean it out by blowing into it. The pepper flew into his face and eyes. He yowled in pain. My husband and I felt terrible and couldn't help him fast enough. Our efforts to wash his eyes out with warm water weren't enough. He kept crying, and we ended up taking him to the hospital. It was such a relief when he was properly taken care of and not suffering anymore.

Most of us would feel that kind of concern when our child is in crisis, wouldn't we?

God had such concern for the Israelites that He sent Moses to rescue them. It took time for the Israelites to learn to trust God. Through the forty years in the wilderness, God performed miracles to help them, and He eventually fulfilled His promise of life in a spacious land, flowing with milk and honey.

Like the Israelites, we are God's children. When we're in pain, suffering physically or emotionally, God will be concerned for us too. Healing may take time, but if we reach out to Him, He will stay with us and help us through.

I know it's hard to believe at times. God can seem far away when we're depressed. Yet He does see us, and He hears our cries when we suffer. In fact, He *feels* our pain and loneliness. Jesus suffered and felt abandoned as He hung on the cross. We can be sure that He, too, understands what we go through. *"As a father has compassion on his children, so the Lord has compassion on those who fear him"* (Psalm 103:13).

We're not alone.

Broken-Hearted

*My sacrifice, O God, is a broken spirit;
a broken and contrite heart you, God, will not despise.*
Psalm 51:17

Have you ever felt really bad about something you've done or the way you've behaved?

It happens to everyone at times. But when our moods aren't stable, we are especially susceptible to feelings of guilt. Sometimes these are well-founded. Sometimes—when we're thinking irrationally—not so. We are often broken-hearted.

I've found that praying Psalm 51 offers great comfort when I'm hurting. David wrote it after he realized how wrong he'd been to commit adultery with Bathsheba and to have her husband killed. David tells God that he has a "contrite [or repentant] heart," that he desires forgiveness and wants to become the person God wants him to be. When I read David's words, I too am able to express my deep regret and pain. I draw closer to God.

Good things come from humbly going to God with a broken and repentant heart. Scripture shows how this can help make us into people God can use.

Take David, for example, as portrayed in Psalm 51. Although great sin had led David to write this prayer, he became *"a man after [God's] own heart"* (Acts 13:22).

And then there's the apostle Peter in the New Testament. Luke 22:61–62 reports that after he denied knowing Jesus three times before His crucifixion, he *"went outside and wept bitterly."* Think of the agony he must have suffered, realizing how he had turned his back on his Lord! He, too, had a broken heart, a heart that was ready to change, ready to obey God. The rest of Peter's story shows a transformed man—a humble yet bold and dynamic speaker who gave his all to Jesus.

If David and Peter were brought closer to God in their brokenness, able to be used by Him, could we not be as well?

Come and Have Breakfast

When they landed, they saw a fire of burning coals there with fish on it, and some bread. Jesus said to them, "Bring some of the fish you have just caught." So Simon Peter climbed back into the boat and dragged the net ashore. It was full of large fish, 153, but even with so many the net was not torn. Jesus said to them, "Come and have breakfast." None of the disciples dared ask him, "Who are you?" They knew it was the Lord.

John 21:9–12

Imagine how the disciples must have felt after such an unfruitful night. First, they're told by a man on shore to put their nets out on the right side of the boat, and they catch all those fish. Then they realize the man is Jesus, welcoming them to "come and have breakfast."

Though a net full of cold slippery fish is impressive, I'm not a fisherman, so that part of the story has never done much for me. What really moves me is the invitation to have breakfast.

After a long night on the water not catching anything, the disciples must have been exhausted and feeling like failures. On top of that, they were grieving an intense loss. Their Lord, whom they had followed for three years, the person on whom they had pinned all their hopes for a new kingdom, was no longer with them.

I think of how it might be for me, after suffering a long dark night of the soul, feeling lost and alone, distant from God. I think of how I might feel in the early morning light, arriving on shore and having Jesus greet me with "Come and have breakfast." The relief, the comfort, the peace, like the embrace of a compassionate friend. Yes, this picture speaks to me. Can you see how the same Jesus who met the disciples onshore two thousand years ago is ready to meet you onshore today?

Christ promises us that He will be with us—at breakfast, lunch, dinner and in between. And after a period of depression, disappointment or loss, it's so good to recognize once more that He is there and He will provide.

Do Not Delay, Lord

But as for me, I am poor and needy; come quickly to me, O God.
You are my help and my deliverer; Lord, do not delay.
Psalm 70:5

Imagine King David kneeling and pleading for help. Imagine someone as powerful as he was openly confessing that he was *"poor and needy."*

Are we, like David, honest enough with God about our struggles? Many of us keep our problems to ourselves. Some of us don't talk to friends and frequently forget to talk to God. We're often too proud to say, "I am poor and needy." Sometimes we don't believe we need help.

Myself? Sometimes, when I journal, I tell God I need Him. But often I try to find a close friend who will understand and have compassion. I long for someone who knows God, a friend who has proven that she cares about me. What I want is comfort from another human being, someone who will be God's hands for me.

The trouble is that friends aren't always available. They often have problems of their own and can't focus on us in the way we wish and need. God is always there, though. We must talk to Him.

But what should we say to God?

Look at the various parts of David's prayer. Note how David lays bare his heart, pleads for urgency and expresses his impatience. When we have trouble finding the words we want, we can read psalms like this one and the many others in our Bible. Psalmists have written prayers we can use. In David we will find a friend. Someone who understands. An instrument of God.

Don't forget God, and don't think He has forgotten you. Don't be afraid to let Him know what you need. You can be sure He'll be listening.

David said, *"You are my help and deliverer."* He recognized that God could be trusted to see him through the crisis. God will see you through yours as well.

Great is Thy Faithfulness

I remember my affliction and my wandering, the bitterness and the gall. I well remember them, and my soul is downcast within me. Yet this I call to mind and therefore I have hope: Because of the LORD's great love we are not consumed, for his compassions never fail. They are new every morning; great is your faithfulness.

Lamentations 3:19–23

One of my favourite hymns is "Great Is Thy Faithfulness," based on Jeremiah's words in Lamentations. When I sing it, I can't prevent the tears from rolling down. What moves me most is how God is faithful to us through the hard times we suffer.

From deep down, where memories of pain reside, we sing—with hope in our hearts—"Great is Thy faithfulness." And how it moves us! We thank God for always being there, rescuing us from our painful struggles and returning us to a life worth living. All we need, He provides. His compassions are new every morning. In every way, this is a song of praise.

Don't you find that we appreciate God's compassionate care for us more than anything when we've suffered and then recovered? And the greater we have suffered, the more this is so. This Scripture, as well as the hymn, was written for people who, like us, have struggled with a lot of difficulties.

We thank God for His provisions in the unfolding of the seasons. A fresh new spring to welcome us, with crocuses and other bulbs coming into bloom, all provided by our faithful creator, God. What a blessing!

Oh that we could stop our busy lives more often and remember God's faithfulness! May we never forget to appreciate all God is, has been, and will be.

Great is His faithfulness!…And, full of hope, we sing, "Strength for today and bright hope for tomorrow, Blessings all [ours], with ten thousand beside!"

Heaven on Earth

Weigela

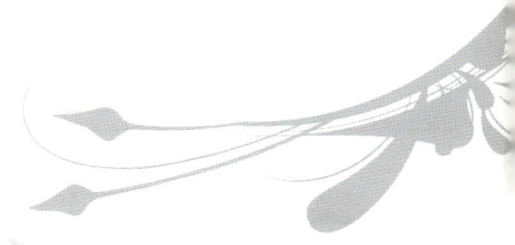

The Lord is my strength and my shield; my heart trusts in him, and I am helped.
My heart leaps for joy and I will give thanks to him in song.
Psalm 28:7, NIV 1984

Have you ever been so overjoyed that you felt your insides dancing? I have. Sometimes I'm so overwhelmed with joy and gratitude that all I can say, over and over, is "Thank You, Lord, thank You." Just as with David, my heart leaps for joy. I'm happy we have the psalms, because they so clearly describe many of the feelings that well up in me, whether it be joy or sadness. Thank God there was David!

Often I've felt as if heaven has arrived on earth. Not everywhere, of course, but within my heart. The way I see it, I'm experiencing the Kingdom of Heaven, the effects of God's rule in the world.

I experience a taste of heaven whenever I study a branch of weigela blossoms up close, admiring it and thanking God for it. I experience heaven when the sun comes out after dreary days of rain. "Thank You, God," I say, and the joyful feeling overtakes me.

Heaven on earth.

Charles Spurgeon said it well:

> *"When Jesus manifests himself to his people, it is heaven on earth;*
> *it is paradise in embryo; it is bliss begun."*[4]

How Great His Love

How great is the love the Father has lavished on us,
that we should be called children of God! And that is what we are!
1 John 3:1, NIV 1984

A friend who was depressed told me she didn't want to live anymore, because she felt unworthy. I considered how I might help her realize she is worthy. I thought, *If only she could find something that would give her life more meaning.* But then I realized I was wrong. A person does not need to have a meaningful life to be worthy.

I believe that we're all—every one of us—worthy in God's sight. All of us who profess that Jesus took our sins on Him are children of God. Yes, *that's what we are!*

I love my troubled friend. I want her to realize how important she is to me, to the many people whose lives she touches, as well as to God. I care about her because she is real with me, seldom pretending to be what she isn't. She shares her pain openly so that I'm given the privilege—through God—to help her carry it. And when she starts to recover, not only is she blessed, we're both blessed. What greater friendship can there be?

When we share openly with God, as my friend does with me, offering Him all we are, we show God that we trust Him. We give ourselves to Him and allow Him to embrace us for who we are. What greater love can there be?

The meaningful things we find to do in our lives make us happy and fulfilled, but they don't make us any more worthy than we already are.

The question we should ask ourselves is not "Am I worthy?" The Bible says that what we need to ask is "Am I loved?" Of course, the answer is yes, we are.

"How great is the love the Father has lavished on us!"

How blessed we are when we allow that love to soak into the depths of our soul. We are worthy and we are loved. Nothing can change that.

How Long, Lord?

Rhododendron in winter

How long, LORD? Will you forget me forever? How long will you hide your face from me? How long must I wrestle with my thoughts and day after day have sorrow in my heart? How long will my enemy triumph over me? Look on me and answer, LORD my God. Give light to my eyes, or I will sleep in death, and my enemy will say, "I have overcome him," and my foes will rejoice when I fall. But I trust in your unfailing love; my heart rejoices in your salvation. I will sing the LORD's praise, for he has been good to me.

Psalm 13

A friend pointed me to this psalm when I was experiencing a long, deep depression that didn't want to lift. Aren't most depressions like that? They seem to last forever, and we find it hard to believe we'll ever feel good again.

Do you feel that way now? If you do, then think about spending some time with Psalm 13. It helped me through some very bad times. Maybe it will do the same for you.

What a relief to hear David cry out to God, *"How long, LORD? Will you forget me forever?"* The words remind me that we're not alone with our deep feelings. Even David, the man close to God's heart, had dark emotions as we do. I gain comfort from that, and I expect all of us suffering from depression will be comforted.

King David shows his honesty, feeling as if the pain will last forever, crying out to God, weeping. He shows that asking God some tough, seemingly disrespectful questions is a normal response to suffering. We're presenting ourselves to God as human beings—with Him.

As you'll see in many of his psalms, David teaches us to follow our expressions of pain with positive reflections about who God is. In the last verses, David encourages us to have faith: *"But I trust in your unfailing love…"*

When we have wept awhile, it's time to take the focus off ourselves and turn it onto God. It's time to remember what He has done for us and to sing His praises. *"For he has been good to [us]."*

What comfort to know that a cold, dark winter never lasts forever. Spring *will* come again. The rhododendron proves it.

"I Don't Want to Lie Down!"

The LORD is my shepherd, I shall not be in want. He makes me lie down in green pastures, he leads me beside quiet waters, he restores my soul.
Psalm 23:1–3, NIV 1984

"I don't *want* to lie down! I don't *want* to rest!" I protest.

The leader of my small group studying this psalm looks startled. This is not what she expected from me, but I continue, "I have things to do. I don't *want* to lie down beside quiet waters."

For those of us living with bipolar disorder, this sentiment might sound familiar. We have periods of super-activity. We need less sleep and accomplish a lot—as long as the mood doesn't go out of control. We are on a high—manic for some, hypomanic (or somewhat high) for others.

One of the problems we experience is overstimulation. Something I read by Charles Spurgeon got me excited. I found it so beautiful that I read it to several friends, eagerly telling them how wonderful it was. Their response was flat. No one got it, and I was disappointed. I thought to myself, *Am I crazy?*

The truth is, I *had* been having some manic symptoms. My sleeping pattern was abnormal, with few periods of uninterrupted sleep. I was waking up and staying up as early as two in the morning and not feeling there was anything wrong with that. Thankfully, I started recognizing what was happening to me. I listened when people who understood pointed out the symptoms: high frustration when I wasn't understood; excitability in my speech; a constant flow of ideas leading to more creativity than usual.

When we experience these moods, we don't want to stop the good feeling. Our friends and family can see that something is wrong, though. They find us too talkative and can't keep up with the many ideas we come up with. We become uncharacteristically impatient, even belligerent, with those closest to us. Some of us buy things we will never need or plan irrational schemes. Our family urges us to get medical help, but we think we're fine and resist. We go higher and higher, sometimes out of control.

God doesn't want this for us. He wants us to stay in step with the rest of the world. As a good shepherd knows the needs of his sheep, so our Heavenly Shepherd knows our needs. In His love for us, our Shepherd wants to make us lie down, calmly and safely. We need to listen to Him, surrender to Him, trust that He knows best.

Listen. Surrender. Trust.

When we listen to our Shepherd, when we let Him lead us beside quiet waters, He *will* restore us. Slowly but surely, we will regain the comfort and calm that a good night's sleep can bring.

Having gone through this many times, I've learned that there's nothing as fantastic as being solidly grounded. Today—at this moment—lying down in green pastures for a rest is fine with me. May I return to rest often.

Light in the Darkness

*In him was life, and that life was the light of all mankind.
The light shines in the darkness, and the darkness has not overcome it.*
John 1:4–5

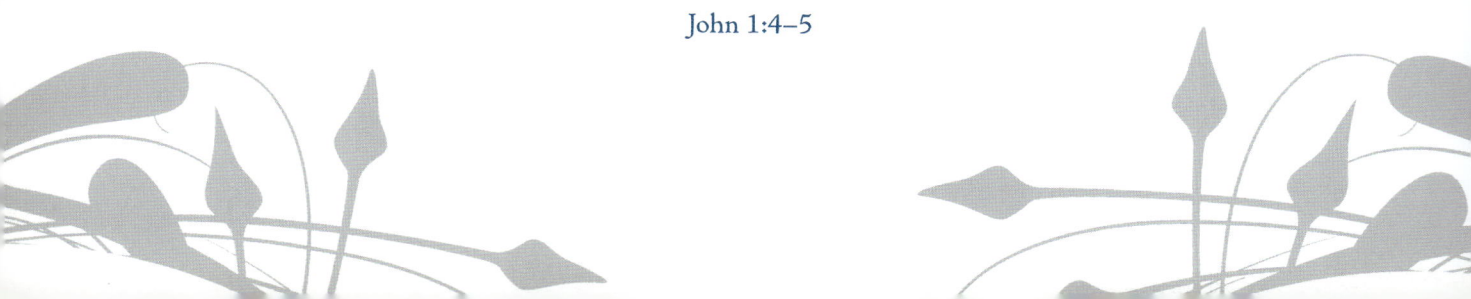

In her book *The Hiding Place*, Corrie ten Boom tells the true story of how she and her family risked their lives hiding Jewish people in their Amsterdam home during the Second World War. She wrote about how they were discovered and how she and her sister Betsie were taken to Ravensbruck, one of the worst concentration camps in Germany.

The camp was a horrendous place. Food rations were half a pound of bread and half a litre of soup per day. The women were made to work hard, and they often suffered from swollen legs and constricted circulation. The stench of burning flesh frequently hung over the camp, reminding them that they too might at any time be gassed and burnt. The inhumane conditions made the women fight, curse, shove, claw and kick each other.

Fleas were so thick in Corrie and Betsie's bunkroom that they swarmed the women entering at the end of the day's work. Yet those fleas turned out to be a blessing.

Corrie and Betsie had managed to smuggle a Bible into the camp, an act that would have meant execution if they had been found out. In the evening they read the Bible, gathering strength and comfort from it. Eventually, they learned that they could read the forbidden book without being detected. The guards didn't check on them, because they didn't want to enter the bunkroom full of fleas.

Gradually, groups of women started gathering in the evening to study God's Word, taking turns reading aloud and praying together, always expressing their gratitude for the fleas that allowed them this freedom to worship. Thanks to the Bible readings, a new atmosphere developed amongst the women. They became kinder towards each other, more polite, more caring.

Betsie began talking to her sister about a plan. "We must go everywhere and tell everyone. There is no pit so deep that God's love is not deeper still." Because of how God's light of love had shone so brightly there at Ravensbruck, she knew that people would believe.

Even in a concentration camp, the darkest, most evil place we can imagine, God's light shone through and lives were changed. Even there... or maybe *especially* there?

God's love can penetrate our darkness too, whether it's the night within us or the night surrounding us. It's amazing how His Word often rings more clearly and powerfully during times of pain and struggle.

"The light shines in the darkness, and the darkness has not overcome it."

Lighting a Candle in the Night

If you spend yourselves in behalf of the hungry and satisfy the needs of the oppressed, then your light will rise in the darkness, and your night will become like the noonday. The L*ORD* *will guide you always; he will satisfy your needs in a sun-scorched land and will strengthen your frame. You will be like a well-watered garden, like a spring whose waters never fail.*

Isaiah 58:10–11

Some years ago, during a deep depression, I offered to do a favour for a friend. This was not easy at the time, but I knew I had to try to be less self-consumed. Thinking about someone else's needs might help me forget my own.

As it turned out, my friend did not need my help. But something happened inside me. A spark had been lit, a small brightening in the darkness I'd been living with. Just the thought of doing something for someone else had made a difference to my mood.

I meditated on this spark. In a few days I would be leading a support group, and I thought what a good thing this would be to share. I planned how I would present this coping strategy, looking for Scripture to back me up and a photograph to illustrate. Lo and behold, over the course of the week, that little spark grew to a steady flame. A candle was burning in the middle of my night.

That candle stayed lit all week. On Friday the devotional I presented described my journey, inspiring the members of the group.

Yes, as Isaiah said, my light did rise in the darkness. Yet it was only a brief reprieve. As you know, the night of depression does not so quickly and easily become like noonday.

I did learn, though, that reaching outside myself to others is a powerful tool against depression. It might not always be the magic answer, but it helps a great deal. Focusing on the needs of others instead of our own, I have found, helps us have a healthy, satisfying and happy life.

Mystery Tour

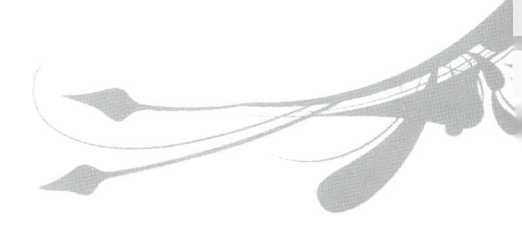

Let the morning bring me word of your unfailing love, for I have put my trust in you.
Show me the way I should go, for to you I entrust my life.
Psalm 143:8

This prayer reminds me of how I felt as a young preschooler when my mother took me on shopping excursions. She led me by the hand through busy streets, weaving her way in the crowds.

I had no idea where Mom was taking me, but that was all right. It was her job to take me and my job to hold her hand tightly and follow along. Mom was in charge, and she would look after things. In my young mind, I didn't know or understand the destination, but that didn't matter. I trusted her.

David must have felt a little like me, learning to trust as he wrote this prayer while being persecuted by his son Absalom. He was afraid, but like a child looked after by his mother, he believed God would show him where to go and what to do next. He trusted that God was in charge.

What comfort it must have been for David to write this prayer! What comfort it could be for us if, like David, we prayed like this, not only during times of trouble, but anytime. What a relief not to have to worry but to place our lives in God's hands, trusting that He will watch out for us! If we could say "Show me the way I should go," where might God take us?

God has taken me on some wonderful mystery tours, to places I could never have imagined. He took me from being a patient in a psychiatric hospital in 1965 to a published author and photographer and the leader of a mental health support ministry. In 1965, the medical staff gave me little hope for a normal life. That's the kind of thing God can do.

Amazing!

On Wings Like Eagles

Even youths grow tired and weary, and young men stumble and fall; but those who hope in the LORD will renew their strength. They will soar on wings like eagles; they will run and not grow weary, they will walk and not be faint.

Isaiah 40:30–31

Isn't it great to see an older person with a youthful spirit having fun? Aches and pains forgotten. Living in the moment. I'd like to be that way, especially as I get older.

How I would love to forget the symptoms of my disorder and the side effects of the meds I take! I want to live while caring for my body and mind but not worrying too much about them. I'd like to live wholeheartedly, hoping in the Lord, renewing my strength, finding interesting and exciting things to do. Don't we all want this?

Many of us, young and old, feel burdened by physical and mental health problems. Life becomes hard to cope with. We are forced to adjust our lifestyle—sometimes a lot. But even when things look bad, a positive approach is possible.

Joshua Prager, a writer who was left hemiplegic after an accident at age nineteen, inspired me greatly. He said, "What makes most of us who we are most of all is not our minds and not our bodies and not what happens to us, but how we respond to what happens to us."[5]

It's how we respond that matters! How encouraging that is! Because of my attitude, I had almost forgotten this universal truth.

We have wonderful examples of people who responded well to their challenges and whose lives have left a lasting impression. Remember Terry Fox, the young Canadian who lost a leg to cancer but ran 5,400 km partway across Canada? He raised $24.7 million for cancer research with his courageous attempt. Then there is Nick Vjuicik, born without arms or legs. His sense of humour and positive messages of hope are an inspiration to many.

Many people who lived with bipolar disorder have left their mark on history too. Try googling "famous people and bipolar" and you'll find a long list. They include Vincent van Gogh, Lord Byron, Rosemary Clooney, Jesse Jackson Jr. and Mel Gibson.

It all depends on how we respond.

There are many people to encourage us, including elderly people who kept right on going in spite of their age. Michelangelo was still producing masterpieces at eighty-nine. In Joshua 14:7–13, we read how Caleb wanted to enter the Promised Land even though he had reached eighty-five. He was eager to do God's will.

Is that the secret? Is that where strength in weary people comes from? Enthusiasm to do what God wants them to do?

What could our own response to life be, despite the problems we face? How could we, with God's help, renew our strength? The answer will be different for each of us. We are unique, each with our own set of gifts. All we have to do is learn what God wants us to do with them. Ask Him and listen to what He tells you.

Let's get excited about life and discover the many things waiting for us to do. God has much to offer—even with our challenges. In this hope we'll find strength.

Patient Endurance

Patient endurance is what you need now, so that you will continue to do God's will. Then you will receive all that he has promised.

Hebrews 10:36, NLT

The tulip bulb spends many months in the ground, preparing to bloom. All this time it is patiently developing to become what God intends it to be.

This reminds me of the long periods of dark depression some of us go through. Scripture tells us that these are only for a while. God is preparing us for something—Malachi 3:3 tells us, *"He will sit as a refiner and purifier of silver."*

Would you be able to endure the suffering better if you knew that God was using that time to prepare you for something? Trials refine us, develop us, make us into people we could never be if life were easy. We need to be patient, not anxiously looking for deliverance from pain.

I like the story of Joseph. Thirteen years passed between the time his brothers sold him into slavery and the time he became second in command in Egypt. Thirteen years of patient endurance—and many trials. Finally he became the person God could use. Under his leadership, Egypt was able to store away enough grain to save many from hunger.

Joseph's brothers came asking for the grain they so badly needed, not realizing whom they were asking. When they found out that the man was their brother, they were petrified.

"But Joseph said to them, 'Don't be afraid. Am I in the place of God? You intended to harm me, but God intended it for good to accomplish what is now being done, the saving of many lives'" (Genesis 50:19–20). Everything that happened to Joseph had a purpose, though neither he nor anyone else could see it at the time. Joseph patiently endured those many years, having faith and loving God. He trusted God's plans, though he could not see what they were.

The difficulties God brings our way also have a purpose, though we may not see it now. We don't have to know why we suffer. Joseph didn't know. Endure patiently, trust God and have faith. If you love God, everything will work together for good, even the difficulties and the suffering (Romans 8:28).

How would things be for you today if your life had been easier? How have your trials refined you?

Raindrops on Roses

You, God, are my God, earnestly I seek you; I thirst for you, my whole being longs for you, in a dry and parched land where there is no water…I will praise you as long as I live, and in your name I will lift up my hands. I will be fully satisfied as with the richest of foods; with singing lips my mouth will praise you.

Psalm 63:1, 4–5

I love to photograph flowers, especially after they've been freshly washed by a shower. That's when they look their best, all dressed up with sparkling jewels.

God and the joy He brings are like thirst-quenching raindrops to a wild rose. When we reach out to Him, spend time with Him, talk with Him, worship and praise Him, He can put sparkle into our everyday lives.

It starts with a craving—a hunger and thirst for God.

I've been thinking a lot about these longings and have come to see that there's joy in this kind of hunger and thirst. Joy because the Bible promises that God waits for us, ready to satisfy our needs. When our appetite is big and healthy, it's great to be fed well.

And yet, what happens when we don't have an appetite? When we sit over our dinners unable to put fork to mouth? It can be hard to reach out when all we want to do is hide from the world. We cry without tears, hoping to find relief. Our valley is dry. Our throats are parched. We see no hope—and long simply to leave the dark place we find ourselves in.

What happens then?

I know from experience that God is waiting patiently in the wings. He does not forget us. He understands what we're going through and shares our pain. His love knows no bounds and is there for us, even in the depths of our despair. We may not feel love at the time, but we can be sure it *is* there.

If we wait patiently, our longing for God our Father will return. We will be blessed with glorious relief from hunger, thirst and weariness.

There *will* be a time when our thirst is quenched. Much as this rose feels the raindrops, we will feel the joy of God with us again. Freshly washed, our lives will meet a new morning.

Singing When You Don't Feel Like It

The crowd joined in the attack against Paul and Silas, and the magistrates ordered them to be stripped and beaten with rods. After they had been severely flogged, they were thrown into prison, and the jailer was commanded to guard them carefully. When he received these orders, he put them in the inner cell and fastened their feet in the stocks. About midnight Paul and Silas were praying and singing hymns to God, and the other prisoners were listening to them.
Acts 16:22–25

Would I be able to sing while in prison and tied down? Would I be able to praise God in song while enduring such a trial? I doubt it. Not while in such pain, in such a place, with only one other person to keep me company.

What a wonder that Paul and Silas could sing after being beaten and locked up in a dark cell! What hymns were they singing? What did the songs of the early Christians sound like? I've often wondered.

There's one thing for sure. Paul and Silas were singing songs of praise. Probably joyfully, probably loudly, because the other prisoners were listening.

Although the music and words would have been different from anything we sing today, they would have expressed the same joy and confidence as some of the worship songs we sing in church today. We praise God, our spirits rising as we reach out to God…I love singing these song, but I'm not so sure I could sing them when I'm in a bad place, in trouble, or in pain.

When I was young, I loved singing with my sister while we did the dishes. I don't have the lung capacity to do that anymore, perhaps because I don't practise enough. At church, led by a worship team and surrounded by friends, I can manage. There, my voice is safely hidden. Yes, I usually sing at church, no matter what I'm going through. Away from church, though, it's difficult. I expect it's like that for many of us.

Let's ask ourselves these questions: Most of us can sing on Sunday, but can we sing on Monday? It's not hard to sing surrounded by others, but can we sing when we're alone? We can sing in the sanctuary, but can we sing in the street? Can we sing when we're in trouble or in pain?

Can we, like Paul and Silas, sing God's praises with confidence and hope?

There have been occasions—and maybe you can relate—when I was unhappy and not able to join in the singing at church. I just listened. Other times, the words brought tear-filled emotion, though I couldn't always tell whether it was joy or sadness. Looking back, I felt close to God in the midst of those tears. Singing hymns and worship songs can do that to us. It can bring us into a closer relationship with God. Such weeping is nothing to be ashamed of.

I wish I could sing while washing dishes. I wish I could praise God in song at my home, as I do at church. I'm going to try. I'm going to go to YouTube and have it keep me company. It's so much easier to sing with someone else, even if it's a recording. I believe I *can* worship God at home, even on a Monday morning. And I bet God will come close when I do. Want to join me?

Talking to God About Joy

And let us run with perseverance the race marked out for us, fixing our eyes on Jesus, the pioneer and perfecter of faith. For the joy set before him he endured the cross, scorning its shame, and sat down at the right hand of the throne of God.

Hebrews 12:1–2

Why does the Bible say so much about joy in the midst of struggle? I've heard this in church but have had trouble grasping it. Two years ago I talked it over with God in this piece. I hope this prayer and God's answer will help you understand better, as it did me:

Lord, I'm confused. Every time I think I've sorted things out, someone or something tells me I haven't. Yet I'd like to be clear about this. How can I pass understanding on to others if I don't have it myself?

My pastor said, "Our attitude in the face of hardship and suffering reflects our confidence in God." He was talking about the joy expressed in Paul's letters from prison. Joy in spite of hardship.

This started me thinking about the depression my friends and I often face. How can an attitude of joy be possible at times like that, when all you want to do is die?

Does my pastor think I don't have confidence in You, Lord, when I'm in the midst of depression? In my own defense, I consider myself a fairly good follower of Christ. Can I help it when depression comes upon me? Can I help it when all I can do is think negative thoughts? I remember with compassion the people in my support group who feel at times that You have abandoned them. Their pain is immense.

I've bravely thought how I need to go through depression once in a while to do the work You have given me to do—to follow my calling to support people like me who have a mood disorder. It's true: because I myself have struggled with depression, I know how to be a good supporter and advocate. I suppose this has given my life meaning. Joy, even?

Yet, over the last couple of years, my experience with depression and the desire to die has been worse than ever. In those times, it was impossible to have an attitude of joy. Even when the episodes passed, I wondered if the benefits were worth what I paid.

Am I thinking of myself too much, Lord? The central purpose of Paul's life was You and his desire to serve You. He wasn't concerned about himself. I would like to be like Paul. I, too, want to serve You. The purpose of my life is not me or my own well-being—at least I try not to let it be. But maybe it is too often.

And You, Lord? Isn't it You I need to look to most of all?

You endured unimaginable suffering as You hung on the cross. You also felt abandoned, crying out, **"My God, my God, why have you forsaken me?"** (Matthew 27:46). No joy there, was there? Yet You willingly endured the cross for the joy set before You (Hebrews 12:2). You knew the good it would do: the transformation, or redemption, of humanity.

So, if I'm truly Your follower in every way, fixing my eyes on You, shouldn't I willingly endure depression, my cross, knowing it will eventually help me have greater compassion for others? It will enable me to help others in ways I otherwise couldn't. In that there is joy.

Lord, help me have the courage to withstand future episodes when they come…because they will always come. Help me follow You wholeheartedly, joyfully, even when it hurts.

The Potter

Woe to those who quarrel with their Maker, those who are nothing but potsherds among the potsherds on the ground. Does the clay say to the potter, 'What are you making?' Does your work say, 'The potter has no hands'? Woe to the one who says to a father, 'What have you begotten?' or to a mother, 'What have you brought to birth?'
Isaiah 45:9–10

―――――――

Years ago, I took a pottery class and found that working the clay was a lot harder than I expected. Getting the walls of the pot the right thickness and making it attractive required work. I created a lot of rejects, returning them to a lump and starting over again. Making truly good pots takes a lot of skill.

Since I was a novice, my pots did not turn out well. They were clumsy and heavy and didn't look good. Yet I felt attached to them. I still have a small one on my bedside table, holding pens and manicure scissors. After all those years, I still remember the thrill of shaping it, of creating something out of a lump of wet, nondescript material.

God, the Master Potter, has no such problems. He makes us exactly as He intends us to be. Sometimes we get angry with God for making us the way He did. We feel like defective goods—a mistake. We lose hope, wondering if we'll ever be useful for anything.

But the Bible tells us not to argue with God or question the way He has made us. God is a skilful creator. He knows what He's doing. Besides, He's not finished yet. As long as we live on this earth, He will continue forming us, helping us become better and better, until we are the best we can be, ready to continue our life with Him.

I wish we could accept ourselves the way God made us and be thankful for the unique gifts He has bestowed on us. I wish we could allow ourselves to be soft clay in His hands, obedient to His moulding. Throughout our lives, He will continue to work with us, helping us become unique. Each one of us is a special piece of handiwork for Him.

Being soft clay in the Master Potter's loving and skilful hands will ensure we are shaped exactly into the kind of person He wants us to be. God doesn't create rejects.

This is Joy

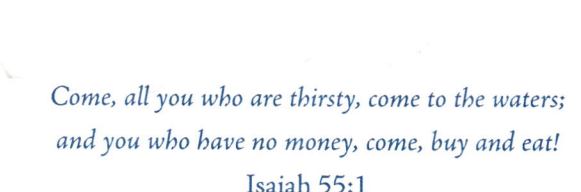

Come, all you who are thirsty, come to the waters;
and you who have no money, come, buy and eat!
Isaiah 55:1

You will go out in joy and be led forth in peace;
the mountains and hills will burst into song before you,
and all the trees of the field will clap their hands.
Isaiah 55:12

What wonderful imagery! Mountains bursting into song, trees clapping their hands. Such an amazing promise of joy God has for us! Not only in what we feel within, but what we see all around us—in nature, in our community, in our relationships. Can there be any greater expression of delight and wonder? Can there be any greater happiness?

These verses were an encouragement to the Jews living in exile in Babylon. Today they speak to everyone who responds to His call to come and quench their thirst. Our awesome God speaks to all of us.

God invites us to receive from Him the rich and meaningful life we need. He offers us *real* life. He promises an everlasting relationship with us. Without cost, He will satisfy our deepest longings.

Who Am I?

But Moses said to God, "Who am I, that I should go to Pharaoh…?"
Exodus 3:11

*Moses said to the L*ORD*, "Pardon your servant, Lord. I have never been eloquent, neither in the past nor since you have spoken to your servant. I am slow of speech and tongue." The L*ORD *said to him, "Who gave human beings their mouths? Who makes them deaf or mute? Who gives them sight or makes them blind? Is it not I, the L*ORD*? Now go; I will help you speak and will teach you what to say."*
Exodus 4:10–12

Wasn't Moses stubborn?

Don't we all, at times, have insecurities and doubts about ourselves? Just like Moses? I did for years and often still do. We may think we're weak, too busy, scared, tired, dumb, a failure, hopeless. We may think our emotional problems are such that we can't do anything of value. It's true, our disorders can handicap us in many ways.

When we feel that nudge from God to do something, do we say to Him, maybe too easily, "Who am I? Don't you remember, God, I have problems that make it hard to do things? I shouldn't have to do this. *Please send someone else*"?

We're no different than Moses. We fear to live the life God intends for us. Yet I know there are always things we can do—big things, little things.

In the passages quoted, Moses thought he was operating under his own power. He didn't realize that God was with him and would be in charge. Moses didn't have to do what he was asked all on his own. He was doing God's work, and God would give him the strength he needed.

Jesus said, *"My grace is all you need. My power is strongest when you are weak"* (2 Corinthians 12:9 NIRV). Moses did come to realize that all things are possible with God, and from that he became a great leader. We have so much to learn from his story.

What is God prompting you to do today?

Endnotes

1. Rick Warren, The Gathering on Mental Illness and the Church, March 2014, Saddleback Church.

2. David Steindl-Rast, Gratefulness, the Heart of Prayer (New Jersey: Paulist Press, 1984).

3. John Piper, "The Pleasure of God in the Good of His People," March 1, 1987, http://www.desiringgod.org/sermons/the-pleasure-of-god-in-the-good-of-his-people.

4. Charles Spurgeon, Morning and Evening (Grand Rapids, Michigan: Zondervan, 1948).

5. Joshua Prager, "In Search of the Man Who Broke My Neck," http://www.ted.com/talks/joshua_prager_in_search_for_the_man_who_broke_my_neck.

Marja Bergen has lived with bipolar disorder since 1965. She accepted Christ as her Saviour twenty years later, realizing she could not live without Him.

In 1999 Marja's book *Riding the Roller Coaster* was published, the beginning of her efforts to reduce the stigma held towards those living with mental health problems. This was followed in 2008 by her second book, *A Firm Place to Stand*, which shows fellow Christians that anyone can have a mental illness, even *with* a close relationship to Jesus Christ. She has written many articles from the perspective of a Christian living with mental health problems, all trying to reduce stigma in the faith community and trying to encourage those who live with such problems.

Living Room, the peer support ministry Marja founded in 2006 has met with much success. Thanks to the publication of manuals as well as media attention, news about *Living Room* spread. This ministry quickly gained recognition as an effective model for faith-based assistance for people with mental illness. Living Room is now part of Sanctuary Mental Health Ministries. (www.sanctuary-ministries.com)

Marja realized that she found great fulfillment supporting others through her writing. So in early 2013, she began sending out devotionals via email to the many contacts she had made over the years with people wanting support. Being an avid photographer, she started including her photographs with these mailings. These emails have led to the publication of this book.

Marja lives in the Vancouver area with Wes, her husband of forty-five years. They have a son, Cornelius and daughter-in-law, Jeannette.

Visit Marja's website at www.marjabergen.com

Also by Marja Bergen

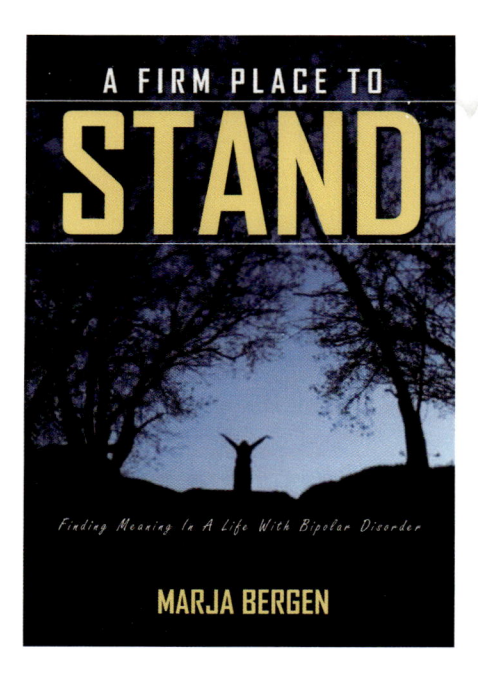

A FIRM PLACE TO STAND

Finding Meaning In A Life With Bipolar Disorder

MARJA BERGEN

9781897373453

A Firm Place to Stand is a must-read for Christians who struggle with mental health challenges and the faith communities who minister to them. In her sincere and candid style, Marja Bergen reflects on her forty-two years with bipolar disorder, showing how faith in God can help a person with a serious illness turn weakness into strength. She describes how God transformed her from an insecure, withdrawn person into a leader, an activist, and the founder of *Living Room*, the growing Christian support group for people with mood disorders.

Word Alive Press, 2008.

Also by Marja Bergen

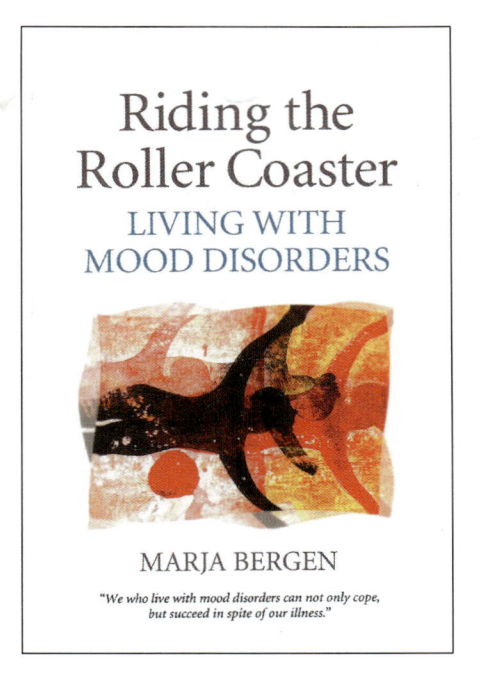

Riding the Roller Coaster
LIVING WITH MOOD DISORDERS

MARJA BERGEN

"We who live with mood disorders can not only cope, but succeed in spite of our illness."

9781896836317

Riding the Roller Coaster is Marja Bergen's first-person account of manic depressive (bipolar) illness. The book is filled with encouragement for those managing mood disorders. It delivers understanding, insight and very tangible strategies on how to overcome the difficulties of depression and manic depression. Marja gives us a very human perspective drawn from her experiences. Her path to recovery is exciting and positive.

Published in 1999, Northstone Publishing.